bearings

b_earings

poems

Karthika Naïr

HarperCollins *Publishers* India

a joint venture with

New Delhi

First published in India in 2009 by
HarperCollins *Publishers* India
a joint venture with
The India Today Group

HarperCollins *Publishers*
A-53, Sector 57, Noida 201301, India
77-85 Fulham Palace Road, London W6 8JB, United Kingdom
Hazelton Lanes, 55 Avenue Road, Suite 2900, Toronto, Ontario M5R 3L2
and 1995 Markham Road, Scarborough, Ontario M1B 5M8, Canada
25 Ryde Road, Pymble, Sydney, NSW 2073, Australia
31 View Road, Glenfield, Auckland 10, New Zealand
10 East 53rd Street, New York NY 10022, USA

Typeset in 11/14 Aldine
InoSoft Systems

Printed and bound at
Thomson Press (India) Ltd.

For Swarup B.R. and Pramod K.G.
My cardinal points
Catalysts at odd hours

Contents

Virga

Damaged Goods

Terra Infirma

bearing (bâr'ĭng) n. 1. The manner in which one carries or conducts oneself: *the poise and bearing of a champion.* **2. a.** A machine or structural part that supports another part. **b.** A device that supports, guides, and reduces the friction of motion between fixed and moving machine parts. **c.** The act, power, or period of producing fruit or offspring. **d.** The quantity produced; yield. **3.** Something that supports weight. **4.** The part of an arch or beam that rests on a support. **5. a.** The act, power, or period of producing fruit or offspring. **b.** The quantity produced; yield. **6.** Direction, especially angular direction measured from one position to another using geographical or celestial reference lines. **7.** Awareness of one's position or situation relative to one's surroundings. Often used in the plural: *lost my bearings after taking the wrong exit.* **8.** Relevant relationship or interconnection: *Those issues have no bearing on our situation.* **9.** Heraldry A charge or device on a field.

adj. Architecture. Designed to support structural weight: a bearing wall. [Origin: bef. 900; ME beren, OE beran; c. OS, OHG beran, D baren, OFris, ON bera,
Goth bairan, G (ge)bären, Russ berët (he) takes, Albanian bie, Tocharian pär-, Phrygian ab-beret (he) brings, L ferre, OIr berid (he) carries, Armenian berem, Gk phérein, Skt bhárati, Avestan baraiti; < IE *bher- (see -fer, -phore]

—The American Heritage®
Dictionary of the English Language, Fourth Edition

VIRGA

There are words that come into our lives like predestined lovers, the shock, the delight of that first meeting lingering—the knowledge that they exist seems to transform the world, at least for a few dizzying moments. Meeting *virga* reaffirmed my faith in language, in its ability to capture what one thought so intensely personal that nobody else would mull over it. The word seemed to describe much more than a precise geological phenomenon; it held shades of the reaction—indefinable, thought-altering, inevitably ephemeral—when faced with a performance. When the body becomes sculptor, clay, plinth, model and work. Constantly dissolved and recomposed.

The attempt to capture the kinetic in words is somewhat like freezing a raindrop in mid-air. Before it changes shape. Before it merges with the earth. Often futile. And at best partial, the change of location from memory's degradable case to a more durable, if just as subjective, one.

These poems are also a memo to the self for insane days. Days that are a raucous bazaar where budgets and figures run headlong into contracts and royalty negotiations, where visa applications and red-taped-tangles with a dozen countries play truant with malfunctioning sets and lost props, and general foul-temperedness (one's own, more often than not) breeds like rodents. A reminder that all this leads somewhere—sometimes, not where it was meant to; to some rather odd places, from time to time. But that it never stays still. Movement, in a word. Or life.

Zero Degrees: Between Boundaries

I met them first in a land where borders
get blurred; where day rises before night's end
and water morphs into high, brumal walls.
A warrior and a monk, two beings—
flanked by shadows that grow and roam at will—
cross-legged in thought, carving with four hands

arabesques on force, loss, fear—close at hand
—and some big runes—selfhood, death—that border
waking hours, and shape dreams against my will.
Their words whirl in unison to the ends
of still skies, etch a tale *of life being*
pruned to papers; of puny men who wall

up futures, then watch unmoved as the walls
and roofs of egos tumble: sleight of hand;
nuke name, nation, calling—the very being
—then revel, leave the body on the border
of reality… the words trail   jerk/ end/
lost in this past, unsure of where they will

be sent next. The shadows step in, strong-willed,
free; spin stretch swallow space and bounce off walls.
Warrior and Monk rise and mirror, end
to end, their shadows who recede and hand
the stage over; drift to the near border
and then vanish like mythical beings.

I leave thoughts on belonging, on being
and the zeroth law that I wilfully
signed, and watch them—one compact, bordering
short; the other pale and spare—vault streaked walls
of culture and kinetic codes. Lock hands
embrace dodge thrust. The duet/duel ends

before I read which is which, if one's end
spells start elsewhere. Threat and trust were being
swirled in synchronized moves till just a hand
was seen, a smudge. Then Warrior's great will
and body juddered to a sudden crash; walled
by a stillness that steals through any border.

Monk departs, a worn being in his hands,
crooning of a day when borders and walls
will cease; midst white shells of spent words, I end.

These experiments in ekphrasis started with *Zero Degrees*, the 2005
duet choreographed and performed by Akram Khan and Sidi Larbi
Cherkaoui. It seemed right that the series 'Virga' should begin and end
with the same. This opening piece, a sestina, took its underlying themes
and the visual lexicon—woven in through the six key words, *borders,
end, walls, being, will, hands*—to create another fable from an incident
that dominates the dance.

Distant Music

(Pierre Henry at the Grande Arche/4 August 2007: impressions)

I. *Overture: The Sun*

Gently disintegrate me: lay me down
on the edge of that frost giant's skull
earthlings call the sky; restore my rings, scour
the shield; then deliquesce my core, Odin,
with the seismic, primal notes your ravens—

Thought and Memory—have retrieved from Time.
First, let me drain phials of chromatic
twilight to sieve heaven of all colour
gently; disintegrate

the blues, the crimson and cream. It is time:
hurl that unerring spear. Let the music
begin; let aurous blood suffuse the earth,
stain the square altar arched skywards, and blot
the columns of crowds gathered to watch me
gently disintegrate.

II. *The Earth's Behest*

I leave this at your ear for when you wake:
a string of amber—carved out from Sol's crest;
scores from my nine worlds on a palimpsest:
Asgard, Midgard, Niflheim … all wrecked to slake
Odin's ire at mortal greed; a flake
of undestroyed desire; one more bequest—
variations from this fading pulse, lest
no legends float on oblivion's lake.

Wear them all: pin the beads on livid locks,
dangle the triads from a grieving ear,
chords on your arm for funeral attire.
Play them forte so other planets shall hear,
comets screech to a halt, and stars shed rocks
when I 'ridesce into sonic bonfire.

III. *Postlude: Dissonant Remains*

Imagine a forest.
$\qquad\qquad\qquad$ No, an ecosystem, entire
in itself, with stunted skyscrapers and sun-worshippers
shrubbing the floor,
$\qquad\qquad\qquad\qquad$ trebles in garnet and sapphire
intertwining chrome spires, a strange breed of bowers.

Add a throng of beasts: mantids on high metal heels
sucking and sampling sound with ribcages, larynxes,
$\qquad$ tongues.
Seventy-eight in a sphere, I counted all the peals
of concrete notes spewed by those giant iron lungs:

snatches of distant music—echoes from lost earth,
the anarchic rhythm of its life, an unsteady breath,
splinters of lustrous tones that had lit up each hearth
—scaling the amplified monophony of death.

No gods, no goddesses, no high priests nor empires remain—
they vanished, each one, into the endless white of the sky.
Beneath smouldering leaves, life opens in spindly refrain.

In 2007, composer Pierre Henry created a commissioned piece *Objectif Terre*, a three-part 'concert-manifesto' retracing the origins of the earth and presaging its disappearance. After Avignon, it was performed at the Esplanade de la Défense near Paris on 4 August the same year. Pierre Henry incorporates geology, Biblical themes and physiological sounds into the piece but the performance, with the composer/conductor towering over the venue, brought to mind something more primeval to this viewer-listener, and my response is grounded in Norse mythology.

At that time, I was working on a writing exercise on riffing from existing poems. Each movement here begins with the opening phrase of a W.S. Graham piece: 'Gently disintegrate me' from 'Enter a Cloud' (1977); 'I leave this at your ear for when you wake' from 'I Leave This at Your Ear' (1970); and 'Imagine a forest' from 'Imagine a Forest' (1977).

Tango for Two and Three-quarters

Dance, you'd said, was not
for unsteady souls. Last night,
Mr Cunningham,
we let them stretch, bend and flex
our minds beyond your decree—

poised on the brittle
wings of an urgent thought: what
of bodies, they asked.
A double duet of eyes—
one set blue, the other brown

(with specks of beryl)—
that soared, dipped and swooped
through a maze of minds,
leaving behind curlicues
of smoking questions as gifts.

Yes, bodies are a
different matter; whether
broken, spent, even
absent—damaged goods that try
to mend, or follow the beat

of souls striding forth
on firm feet to a stage primed
for the strange dyad:
a man who'd stopped walking and
a woman who danced no more.

Heads, limbs and torsos
featured but they're valiant hearts
that took centre-stage
as elisions of flesh shared
hushed backdrops with future ghosts.

An adagio played
on will and a walking-stick
(three-pronged, grey-and-white);
glissades with a motorized
wheelchair for verve, whim and grace;

closed with the embrace
of unborn hope—a tango
for two and three-fourths.
Yes, bodies will dance where souls
hear music in every breath.

These interconnected tanka are for Priscilla Newell and Vincent
Fritschi, whose dance *Not for Unsteady Souls* inspired and informed my
writing, and also my world view. The title of their duet is a reference to
a quote made by choreographer Merce Cunningham: 'Dance is not for
unsteady souls.'

If on a Summer Night in Paris ...

You find yourself held
hostage by a tribe of wild,
unwashed stars—spears in
hand—at the Palais Royal,
mutter the word *flamenco*.

Portals then open
to an ancient alien land
of *cante, palo*
and *baile* where stomping heels
etch out the lines of empire,

an arm extended
carves steles on the wind's broad
back, a sprung longbow
called Israel unleashes
La Edad de Oro, will

galvanize both storm
and mirage on July skies.
But if rain should dare
pierce eyes or attention, plunge
both in the subaqueous

folds of a velvet,
venous voice filling the ground.
And, before you leave,
pluck shadows from the haikus
he's stippled across night's veil.

Another set of tanka, this time on Israel Galván's piece *La Edad de Oro* at
the Paris Quartier d'été festival in July 2007.

Tempus Fugit

I think I would like to die watching you dance,
feet staying quicksilver skies, arms a swift crease
of light across longitudes. Stars rise from trance

at your touch, drape the stage with night while stagehands
mix music (bass from springtides, then soughing trees,
I think). I would like to die watching you dance

this tango with Mistress Time—trellised, by chance
or choice, in memory's arms—, transform a frieze
to light. Across longitudes, she twists in trance

till lips landlocked by your will blaze morning, lance
the inky continent, where—like yestreen breeze—
I think I would like to die. Watching you dance,

scissor land and sea, curve orbits with bare hands,
Time learns to whirl on lone, hennaed feet: release
of light on longitudes. Stars fall into trance

as you plummet out of life: no backward glance
of farewell, no thunder, no tears. With such ease
would I like to die, I think, watching your dance
—like lightning on longitudes—strike and entrance.

'Tempus Fugit' draws on the eponymous 2004 piece choreographed
by Sidi Larbi Cherkaoui. The dance is an expansive ensemble work
that shifts from the Middle Ages to the Pop Years, from Morocco to
a fantasized India to France, spinning time and place like so many
interchangeable tops. The villanelle picks up specific segments and
unravels a thought that snagged while watching a rehearsal …

Rodin While Casting *The Kiss*

Sculpture is the art of hollows and mounds.
Feelings emerge; passion and life vibrate,
flood the surface as Francesca astounds
Sculpture.
              Is the art of hollows and mounds
licensed—in my hands—to break all bounds,
let love reign on Hell's Gates?
                    Yes, for slighting Fate
sculpture is the art. Of hollows and mounds
feelings must surge, passion and life vibrate.

Francesca da Rimini on *The Kiss*

As I seize his starved lips, desire in blithe undress
rises, like the sun, lighting bodies to their core.
Rodin released us from sin, poor souls that transgressed
as I seized his starved lips. Desire in blithe undress
arches my back, love cast in curves will egress
from the shades as high albedo of a new lore.
As I seize his starved lips, desire in full undress
rises, lighting, delighting bodies to their core.

The two triolets are a diptych on Auguste Rodin's sculpture *The Kiss,*
one imagined through Rodin's eyes, and the other through those of
the female protagonist Fransesca de Rimini, a character from Dante's
Inferno murdered by her husband Giovanni Malatesta for falling in love
with his brother, Paolo. In Rodin's version, they are both killed before
the kiss is consummated but maybe there is room for cheer in the fact
that the sculptor subsequently removed them from his *Gates of Hell* for
looking too rapturous.

Four Figurines on a Base by Alberto Giacometti

They stand still and straight through memory's tides:

four women draped in brazen skin and trained
tresses; their jagged shadows pinning me
against the lilac night Paris had served
for supper.

                    Distance stretching between us

like deserts of thought; rising, receding
into seasonal dunes then hardening

to form an unclimbable tor.

                      Small, taller,
tall, smaller, arms akimbo, and feet rooted
in the same burnished silence; they still glance
down at me, eyes kohled with indifference.

Adoration

I

Mrs Rémy next to me
nods and applauds vigorously,
                              flushed
fingers swooping to snatch
each feathered word from the Panditji;
grunts, mutters, smiles
                    in private
discussion, shrugging off the two
thousand eyes and ears jostling
for this rare darshan: he is hers
and hers alone
                    —the priceless
possession frozen as effigy
on her non-flip mobile telephone,
screen-shared with a flattened
elongated Saraswathy.

I turn and stare, her fingers,
her voice treading heavily
on my line of audition;
but the high disdain
                    in this gaze

Music class by Pandit Ravi Shankar at Salle Pleyel, Paris, 2 September
2008.

19

shatters before the sledgehammer
of her bliss
                              —and the face
of a stranger named devotion.

II

Flustered eyes retreat, dive headlong
from the balcony, spin into the stalls,
seeking, sifting through the heads below.
Meanwhile, the master's long alaap
in Memory (major)—moving
from Paris, autumn of thirty-one,
to Maihar, then music's destiny—
soars into jodh beyond the Vindhya
with coloured tales of parent scales
in full octave (all seventy-two).
Dhrupad, dhamaal, khyal, thumri,
a forlorn kajari … come and curtsy.

By the time the taal arrive,
ushered by tongue and tabla
for explanation—
ektaal, teental, rupaktaal
then *khali* to break the flight
(*thihai* and *farmayishen*
scampering in quick succession);

mine eyes have found their station,
alighting—relieved!—on a cherished
crown, still shrapnelled with silver
from the skies, shoulders
shambling towards his seat.
We disbelievers too
have our demigods—
favoured, flawed.

Zero Degrees: Screenshots

Before/

I

Ten minutes to eight:
two thousand feet filing in
a calibrated scramble
lead their wards to the waiting
arms of numbered seats.

II

Seven past the hour,
a thinning of amber air;
the rustle and the murmurs
from several hundred chairs
are blotted to a hush.

III

Dehiscence with the
dimming of the lights: scatter
a dozen usherettes, spores
in pleated black threads,
from aisles towards doors.

IV

Even the debate
in row five—a sibilant spat
over car keys gone awol—
curls up beneath a satin
skirt to hibernate.

the performance

V

Like relics of the future
two white figures lie;
or husks of discarded selves?
Attempts to label dissolve:
their walking mirrors approach,
now gazing with twin furrowed
heads at a near past

And half-lotussed on land's end,
calligraph with voices strong
and pure, fine strokes of thought:
these eyes await, with pages
primed to bear traces even
of unspoken ones.

VI

Here lies the roadmap.
Swap hemispheres, switch
off all certainties: nation
name, residence; weigh
up your humanity, wrap
it in tissue, set
it aside for milder climes.

VII

Journey from Dhaka
to Calcutta; or arrowhead
from life to unbeing, pause
to rub shoulders with
death on the way.

VIII

Identity hubble-bubbles
into uncaring heavens
as colourless fumes.
I clutch at tendrils rising,
grasp perhaps one in my fist.

IX

Death rides the train ticketless
unchecked by my side;
picks at random and departs
clunk, clunk, clunking the chosen
head in counterpoint
to the metallic
pound of tiring wheels.
I trap concern in one hand,
gag conscience with the other
and step away to safety.

X

What is the colour
of my identity? Red like
blood or the cover of a
passport; EU-red to protect
and pre-select—new
caste lines for the planet?

Define me without
numbers; describe me
devoid of codes, colour
and country. Vanish
the red passport, and
what remains of me?
Will specks of this self
survive in your eyes,
or be expelled as
foreign bodies must?

XI

The glissade of one
from prefix *some* to
none hinges on little
and takes only an instant:
seizure of the red booklet;
sponsor of my soul.

XII

Do not gaze into the eyes
of power, do not let them
spot you. Compound eyes, fly-like,
can see clear only when close.
Stay far and fuzzy: do not
exist, do not die.
Do not catch the eyes
of power: dark and empty,
they will mark out, then
stalk, your defiant face.

XIII

I reach out, I touch, wonder:
am I more than merely your
Other? Hands seek trace
brush and enlace yours
tangle with history then
curve in questions
like hybrid anemones:
on labels we score—like 'you'
or 'me'; of where they begin
and whether they end.
Shopworn ones, we know,
but even these don't come
with answers to cut
along dotted lines.

XIV

Dive tumble or vault
thrust parry and flip
higher faster stronger than
you yet find myself
back each time at the starting
block, scrolled to zero.

I slice space with each
successive orbit, leapfrog
limits and watch you
step into my silhouette.

Swap, even swipe, faces;
seek one carved Winner—
only they all weigh
just as much, and bear
price tags for every head.

/ends.

XV

Darkness, with the sound of an
instant distending: unleash
breath, clap eyelids, and retrieve
speech from chasmal depths.

XVI

A sudden rain of light:
applause landslides to the stage,
unearths a bevy of crew
and creators behind white walls.
Curtain calls splinter a roof.

XVII

Return to dormant limbs, the tight
embrace of theatre seats,
the resumed row of neighbours
(with car keys still much at large);
catch lambent flecks of magic
—the snatch of a song, a spin—
carry them home in my eyes
to light up the coming year.

The concluding seventeen senryu-like poems return to *Zero Degrees*,
and are a retelling of a viewer's experience through the seventy-five
minutes of the piece, set as a triptych with a 'before' and 'after' to situate
'the performance' in a continuum. A logbook of six performances across
fifteen months …

DAMAGED GOODS

It is a relief to see this section today as just that: one among several. Because, initially, poetry threatened to be solely an inventory of damage, in its many hues and forms. For reasons that would be too tedious to dwell on, hospitals and related demons featured prominently. Bereavement and absence, immigration policies, loss of memory or love, the assorted bruises of lives around me also clamoured to make an appearance.

Like early alchemists, I attempted to transmute base matter into something else—with plenty of the obligatory explosions in between, ones that leave sooty streaks, singed hair, torn clothes (all quite hilarious when in a comic strip). And, once in a while, that something else did transpire: the episodes behind 'Visiting Hours' actually became funny while reliving them; and reducing pain into a pathological stalker made it—for a brief moment—more a pathetic than a dreaded figure.

'Damaged Goods' has by no means retired; it is just that it no longer occupies centre-stage.

Afterwards

It still feels new, this moment metronoming my days.
Fuzzy-edged, it stretches like a twilight shadow,
while sore eyes adrift on a trolley lift in a haze.

Liveried attendants on wheels speck the weaving space,
blue-green with steel legs and burdens—yes, them I greet,
    though
it still feels new. This moment metronoming my days

returns for the thirtieth time; I wake sliced by blunt rays
hurled from a murky sky whose clouds clog my throat and
    slow
sore eyes adrift on a trolley sifting through a haze,

seeking feet, hands, a human voice, someone in this maze
of steel widgets and sterile breaths to tell me they know
it must feel new, this moment metronoming my days.

My hand, decked with lifelines, reaches a papery face—
mine: a far planet, arid, though streams spurt rust and flow.
Then sore eyes adrift on a trolley peer past the haze

of thiopentane and pain to snag a surgeon's cool gaze;
he rakes my chest, and proclaims to a nurse, 'It will snow.'
Yes, it stays new, this moment metronoming my days,
when sore eyes adrift on a trolley lift in a haze.

Interregnum

Is it day where you are, or does the moon
loiter overhead, watching you like I
used to, tracing with an unsteady breath
those eyes, sleeping brows, the arc of a smile?
Do your hands still stray unbidden at night,
angling to fold my beat within your heart?

It is an odd, wakeful creature, my heart,
tossing gravelly queries at the moon—
as though to smash the murky pane of night
and retrieve a name, a latitude I
seek: the exact location of your smile.
Delhi, Dhaka, I cite under my breath,

Bangkok, Beijing, or up north where the breath
scars the air still, white (like absence a heart):
Vostok, Yukon? Legends that made us smile
once, and contrail maps under a half-moon.
You had checked airline schedules while I
counted cash and clean socks that muggy night.

Your last letter said they woke you at night:
strands of memory that cut off a breath;
roving thoughts you cannot call to heel. I
find those in the mail, addressed to my heart,
dropped by the same russet-tinted moon
wearing faded love bites and a smug smile.

34

Free from nations and rules, that tramp can smile:
no trolled borders lie between her and night!
Not celestial travellers like the moon,
you and I fill up forms, plead, hold our breath;
cling to vagrant hope that an unknown heart
will relent, sign, scrawl ten digits. Then I,

decked in new, numbered dignity, yes! I
could indulge this tropism towards your smile;
rush across to you, blood back to the heart.
Swathed as one in the ample down of night,
we'd learn anew to synchronize the breath
of desire, and shut out the strident moon.

Till then, though, there is just the moon as I
carve with hushed breath the template of a smile,
sword to end the siege of night on my heart.

Inheritance

Five-o-clock sorrow stubbles father's cheeks his eyes
fly swiftly across the room greeting glances with kin
and kith then return like two homing pigeons to rest
on the small silent figure in a handspun white sari lain
(in that room with marble-flecked floor and seven
     windows)
upon a braided coir mat beside a carved bronze lamp
thigh-high all twenty-four wicks on six tiers ablaze
fuelled by fresh coconut oil and husks of early memory
retrieved from half-forgotten teakwood crannies

A kinswoman stretches a hoary hand to smooth a strand
of still-sentient hair flopping across granny's naked face
her face with newly ironed furrows crisp and neat
as the seven starched pleats on her best white handspun
cotton sari edged with gold brocade and blue flowers
she caresses that face abandoned ground now that the
     enemy
who swam up granny's blood hammered holes in her
     mind
melted muscles into mush and carpet-bombed her brain
has decamped after seven-year-long V-day revelry

Far-flung cousins an estranged daughter-in-law
her resident nurse three betel-chewing crimson-lipped
neighbours nephews and nieces a community leader
or two and packs of grand and great-grandchildren

(three to thirteen years of age from pre-school to puberty)
a few former fellow teachers too flit out and in some
feigning sorrow others breathing honest relief gesturing
     orders
checking wrists for holy hours or skipping in infant energy
then tiptoeing past death with confused suddenly caught
     breath

In a far corner her daughters lip wordlessly together
ancient prayers and invoke ageless wayward deities
in a bid for peace and protection as past present and future
merge into a roiled landscape of the known and unknown
litanies for her soul but not without a plea for freedom from
     their
birthright rescue from a legacy that could just swim
up their blood hammer holes in their minds melt muscles
into mush carpet-bomb their brains and chain their
     children
to many-year-long sentences beside desiccating bedsides

Plain Speaking: Serenade of a Stalker

Thirty-three years, two months and seven whirls
of the Earth on ageing toes: I have wooed
her smile through cities, seasons, the spread of
ink beneath those eyes—with all the longing
of an insomniac for sleep's exiled
embrace. Seldom have I let that face bolt

from my gaze. No stakes, locks or windows
with bars could block my path; they should have told
her right at the start: I am what you'd call
the persistent sort. But refined too, I
was sent to the right schools: switch off the stars
before spearing a throat with throbbing tongue;

leave blood-roses by the pillow, after—
or a choker, five ruby welts set in
purple filigree for a slender neck.
Follow firm the old strictures of courtship,
timely reminders, even when apart:
a blank call at breakfast, sweet nothings sent

up blushing veins while at the grocer's ...
an errant heartbeat at noon—an echo
of me in the mirror? Yes, souvenirs
of desire to tell her I'm never far.

Yet my suit lies spurned afresh: she is riled,
and the litany of love's failings long.

I never knock, nor say when I will come.
My constancy robbed her of the suitors
from her youth, my shadow of space to grow.
Thirty-three years, two months and seven whirls
of the Earth on ageing toes: proof of rare
passion, yes, I see you nod. All reduced

to restraining orders, and a black curse
on my head. Starched witches in blue hunt me
with pellets and poison darts; once, they,
with lead-clad kinsmen, strapped me in a hull,
strobed me to smithereens like a mad dog.
But love lingers in pieces, as I do.

The moon may forsake its night oft and on,
but not I my prize: shards are better still
to enter each pore, swim in her waters
and court her thoughts. If possession be nine-tenths
of the law, I rule her breath, blazon
my colours 'cross the frontiers of her skin.

Yet I wait, and wait again, for all my
reign, in the hope of recognition in
a smile, and unclenched eyes to make me whole.

Terra Incognita

Can you hear it? Can you hear my music tonight?
Are you of them whose hearts pound and words dry
On parched spirits as familiar, forsaken notes ignite
Sparks of incarnadine memory, which flare in reply?
Are those your dreams that I invade in the moonlight,
And strains from your plucked veins that rise to the sky?

There are many scores of you, I know, strewn pell-mell
Across the sphere, vagrant drops of an unseasonable
Rainstorm, or seeds fallen on foreign lands. So I dwell
Since defunct then divided, like in some strange fable—
Or rather flit, for want of laws, pennants, port or fell
—In your minds, in nostalgia's arms; the label

Patria—a parachronism—on proud hennaed hands; the
    smell
Of me wafting with walnuts and pinecones, denied
    farewell.

Pillowtalk

Death dropped in for a chat
tonight, bearing a posy of queries and
a furrowed forehead. Perched on my windowsill,
watched me court an undeserving,
inconstant breath, and then smoked
another thoughtful joint.
He's changed a little, since we last met:
quieter, courteous, quaintly
curious; still dangerous.
And the hairdo, i see, is new as well,
with locks as tangled as my existence.
It suits him, though, quite like the fine
cloak of care he's donned to lull me
into ease, prelude to speech.

He wants to know, he says,
the voice [bass not baritone] flecked with wonder,
why i fight a battle lost
long before the bugles were blown; wild causes
were fine, but what was mine?
'What is it you resist? Not me, for I am
no stranger, and have stayed true
since your memory began
tracing slender tributaries through time.'
And then, what rankled: 'Why repugnance, why not
fear? We made a pact: assent from you, and in return,

I would wield possession of your pulse,
train it to throb and leave it on a leash, not long but wide.
But now, I touch a chord of distance,
beats of a heart that drum refusal.'

My eyes close, as his words course
down the years, rinsing recollections, retrieving
moments polished to catch the sun in their curves.
Death does not lie:
he has held my hand, never flinched, not
even when pain-filled fingers clawed sightlessly;
seen impossible dreams find words,
sail out on their wings and light up a starless heaven;
stroked my forehead as infant eyes
learnt the contours of a black, beastly respirator;
hummed limericks next to masked hordes
of surgeons, morphing one theatre
into another, shaping laughs amidst scalpels.
Eleven thousand six hundred and seventy
days of combat on uneven ground.
How would i define him: faithful foe,
lethal ally? i never really asked
for an introduction, didn't
even think of it. And, who, anyway, had time
for dialectics? My adversary was teaching me
to take his leash and gird the globe.

And even in these last months
—since i swapped consent for discontent, migrated
to an unknown land with no safety nets nor air cushions
—he would meet me now and then.

Trysts he inscribed in achromic ink in my agenda.
A glimpse behind the curtain
of acrid smoke and squeals of terrorized
tyres at an intersection.
Just a fuzzy greeting, sometimes, in those last
seconds before the thiopentane raced
to hoist its flag on the brain, and unleash oblivion.
Once, when pain wound bands
—vajra bands, molten lightning—around powerless lungs,
forcing air to abdicate.

Memory ebbs, i see him
through closed eyes, and the sharp fragrance of paprika
nudges my nostrils: the smell of him, then,
remains unchanged through time and territory.
Eleven thousand six hundred and seventy
days of combat on uneven ground.
The truest of adversaries faces me, deserves
no less a gift than truth.
And in the telling, shall i learn it too?
I measure my words, spoonfuls for a pot of tea,
brewed strong and dark but not bitter:
'How can i explain? It wasn't you, nor
the battle—clean, constant, inevitable—
i deserted. It is the arrogance of Fate
whose dictates you will unsparingly obey;
the insolence of a monarch who delights in flooding
sandcastles of desire, in robbing my
resolve: it is that i resent,
and hence resist.
Her last decree, which reaved subjects of the

one power left—the scene of the final battle,
decided me: if i cannot choose,
i will pick up a new arm, deadly: surrender.
Shall triturate the treaties of war,
turn my back, walk away, and it will be the
nape of an indifferent neck your
knife will cleave.'

Death breaks in, courtesy stubbed out
with the joint, 'But what of the honour you sought?
surrender wins no wreaths.
What of your pulse that is bound
by covenant to battle, and knows no other cadence?
What will you do of the years or months
or even instants awaiting my return?'
Hesitantly like a wintry dawn, a path opens
even as he rebukes.
'No honour, true. But why want wreaths:
i shall shatter, when you pluck out
my pulse, into a million iridescent
bits of shrapnel on the same night sky
where we sent my dreams,
and overhang this orb.

'And until then, i shall learn new things:
taste, smell and touch.
maybe wash out others: vigil,
weaponry, vengeance. Try, even, to forget
Fate's caprices, and my calendar.
Eleven thousand six hundred and seventy
days of combat on uneven ground.

But i shall weigh time
no more, just surf its breakers;
catch roasted sunbeams on my tongue;
and breathe the beauty of an airborne acrobat.'

Last Act

Light falters at the doorway, watches

Uneven rows of medicaments patrol
all peripheries: walls, shelves, windowsills;
even check the spread of the floor.

In the outer reaches a bedpan broods, as

Moored to a gravity drip—pecking at air
shredded by a bedside fan—she lies: fading
colour against crisp hospital linen.

Blueprint

Nothing remains …
No edifices, no pillars, not even ruins.
Why write, why remember …
Why keep anything?
Why, a fond visitor, knocking
aloud on my door, with no heed
for niceties, like the time of day
or thought. Will he leave then
if I say: because
the past is not hallowed
land, cleansed, untouched.
Let it be arable, breathing
soil (enriched
by the humus of memories)—
grapnel for my tomorrows.
I shall build.
No turrets to kiss the clouds,
nor crypts to bury slices of life …
perhaps a cottage—thatched
roof, uneven floors, me-sized
windows to let the day in,
night slip out without tripping—
or a hothouse for wild, leafy
hopes. But build
I will.

Visiting Hours/Circa 1989

I. 4 P.M.
No, can't say I know you; nor recall a friendship
from nineteen sixty-six (they hadn't spliced me yet).
But you are family—that's what Achan let slip—,

almost (his third cousin's … nephew back from Tibet?).
He said to welcome you, do take a ringside seat.
I'm here for the long haul—yes, that's the new gullet!

In vulcanized rubber—brick-red—to fight the heat,
woven firmly around what used to be my waist.
They'll unstitch me today; it's meant to be a treat.

Achan? He went to empty the bedpan in haste,
and Amma for a bath. She needs a real sheep dip
after sleeping on this floor—dirt flakes like dried
   toothpaste

—the last fifty-one nights. But this was no planned trip—
unlike yours—with pit stops, friends, and tea with gossip!

II. 5 P.M.
Is that your son, Ma'am? Yes, he is really smart
for not-quite-three-years-old, but he's trying to snatch
I.V. lines from the Port-a-cath that fuels my heart.

I can see he is bored. It's sad he can't play catch
or explore autoclaves: they build wards with scant thought
for young visitors here! The doctor and his batch

of interns are coming (hard day? They look quite taut).
Hie, have the reports come? Drat, you'll unzip my chest?
Wait! Get rid of them first, this solicitous lot

of teachers, toddlers, nuns—and a neighbour's house
    guest,
before the guided tour—complete with photos and chart
—you will begin on my sinking dune of a breast,

drilled with tube wells, watered. Will you say, *this won't hurt*,
or *it won't take long*: worn mantras you must impart.

III. 6.45 P.M.
You are late as usual. They'll soon call it a day:
disconnect the spent sun, transfuse the sky with sleep.
We get fifteen minutes. Must you walk all the way

from school to prove a point? Buses, ricks, your dad's jeep,
all shunned in favour of your newly retrieved feet.
You're right, if I'd spent months yoked to a cast, I'd leap

like Bambi on a trip, turn cartwheels on the street.
Sorry I am scrappy—it's my sixteen-year-old
self, sprung free for the night—but it's so good to greet

someone without a smile! You don't need to be told
how kind it was to come; you aren't going to pray
for my young, shapeless soul. And when your hands
    enfold

mine, hennaed with heparin, it won't be to weigh
the pace of a stray pulse. Yes, I wish you could stay.

In Memoriam

I. *Relics*
You didn't leave much behind when you slipped
silent through some unseen crevice in time.

The scent of a name swiftly rent by tearful
chords (shreds hung in the air, just out of reach).

Biannual torrents of dayspring rites
when payasam and prayer flash-flooded
the neighbourhood—baffling me for nine years …

Shadows from laughing eyes I had found
frozen on cellulose strips (and long thought
were mine) crypted within the covers of
velveteen books on a high, unfriendly shelf.

A three-line memorial in a pale blue file:
life and love scaled to *disease, diagnosis,*
death with date and description, nothing
more—aseptic headstone raised for a ghost
star who didn't leave much behind.

Other remains crowded out yours by and by.
Wordless fury at survival kept under cobalt
paternal lock, bluebeard's chamber that opened
only to one knock;
               glaciers of growing

loss left as moraines on a mother's face;
                                    rising
debris from the link between you and me—
neatly piled beside the same crevice I lose
my way back to, over and over, with no effort at all.

You didn't leave much behind, but nothingness
can expand into a red giant with grief at its core.

II. *Resurrection*

I tried remaking you with swatches of stolen
memory, seaming a harlequin next-of-kin.

First raided the maternal troves: traced
shapes out of mother's soundlessness; snipped
yarn from her three chirpy younger sisters.

I didn't spare granny either, sifting her
cataractal mind for traces of your smile.

(kept clear off the menfolk though: they stood
guard night and day over theirs, buried ten-foot
deep in child and prowler-proof vaults.)

You stayed sketchy, all dots, shades and split
helixes—a silhouette behind a shattered
pane, touching which made thoughts bleed.

So the thieving spread wider and wilder.
I sought your colours, contours all over:

A head among tousled monsoon clouds
your gaze on the burnished afternoon earth
the voice in local summer tides.

The name, the name grew everywhere:
in myths and magazines, or family
trees, fiction, television—any one I chose
could wipe out another possible you.

You walked with me, travelling through
childhood, teenage, voting-right-hood …
I changed templates, crafted new ones through the ride.
Till the time it felt too much like work,
too much a snail within a turtle's shuck.

Unravelled you on land's edge, then watched
my patchwork sibling return to the clouds,
the sun, the sea—and someone's memory.

TERRA INFIRMA

Persistent, impolite questions about the definition of home and identity; the desire to inhabit a space as well as its shadows; the quest for attachment and the parallel one for flight: these seem neither new, nor diasporic prerogatives. Home could be a dubious notion even when one has not changed residence once. Sometimes the tendrils of belonging dig deeper when living out of a suitcase. Sometimes not.

Perhaps in keeping with the changeable, patched ground it sprang from, 'Terra Infirma' also afforded the greatest freedom in form: from villanelle to tanka, rondeau to ruba'i, sestina to sonnet, free verse to concrete poetry, they met up like contacts on Facebook, some familiar faces and others, friends of friends, chance strangers …

Sighting at the Centre Georges Pompidou

As the escalator drifts heavenwards, out of sight,
and Paris recedes below, discreet chiaroscuro in grey;
is it you I glimpse in the waning winter light?

It is hard to tell when one wings to such a height,
features fade, like ageing facsimiles, and eyes disobey.
As the escalator drifts heavenwards, out of sight,

the skyline, it seems, smiles with disdain at my plight.
For it can feel the arrhythmic beat of this inept cliché:
could it be you I glimpse in the waning winter light?

Or a stranger clad in the same face, the weightless delight:
a look when sated, with kisses or a great Dadaist display.
Then the escalator drifts heavenwards, out of sight,

to modern art's turf, terra infirma, where the masters
    incite
me to speak twelve syllables, end this searing disarray:
Is it you I glimpse in the waning winter light?

Rogue memory resurges, puts seven-year oblivion to
    flight,
Shatters sufficiency, amulet that kept pain and joy at bay.
The escalator drifts downwards into the city's sight.
It was not you I glimpsed in the waning winter light.

Soundscapes in Saint-Denis

June tears off the gnarled,
grey caul over the city.
Summer tumbles forth,

squalling, the dismal
afterbirth of cumulus
rinsed out with its rain.

Settlements of sound
spring from clefts in sidewalks, skies:
motile, vibrant burgs;

mall of dialects—
filigreed with earth, fire, frost;
and a pool of hush.

From the Basilica ...

Rib-vaulting notes of Mozart's *Requiem*
rise from the nave,

    soar—past tiers of stillness—
     into the skies and graze
      the brushed bronze

of Grand Corps Malade's voice,
  the load and thrust

of scanned syllables from Café Culture
across the street—Dionysian slammers'
weekly tryst: jousts with metre

         mot

         morpheme.
Passage des Deux Pichets, three beats away:
rollers and skateboarders
d
  i
    p
  s
     y
      -
        d
      o
     o
       d
      l
     e
in
    discordant
glee,

      then cusp with echoes
      of bulimic, clashing caddies in close-by
      Carrefour,
urban temple of our times.

... down streetways ...

In rue Gabriel Péri, wind my way

through colonnades of mobile tongues:
Pushtu.
   Polish.
     Bambara?
       Bengali.
Bracketed by French,
       Flemish,
        Arabic ...
and run smack into a familiar souk:
Quand on n'a que l'amour
       tangled in strains
of *ye jo halka halka soroor hai.*

Both fading before a blaring claret;
Antha arabi kadaloram, aun azhagen kandené...

... then trailing back ...

As the rattle and drum, the grating kiss
of wheel and rail
        —aphotic rock from line
thirteen—
     mosaic the ground
beneath my feet,
   both tugged by thought and tympanum back
to the Basilica for music, mine
to choose:
           Kronos Quartet
cadencing on the night plain,
       or ancient

incantations of Arizonan Indians
—young Pocahontas courting exiled gods?

Monteverdi wins the vote:
the Collegium Vocale Ghent will rouse
this dormitory of the royal dead
          with his *Vespers for the Blessed Virgin,*
                    bathe ears and soul

in a liquid blaze of sound: arcs of ruby,
                    green and gold will spring in the air, imbue
breaths;

                                             fly with

buttresses towards outer walls,
and impale gargoyles gaping in delight.

...before a final pitstop.

Turn right to the rue de Strasbourg—slicing
the cemetery into a Dali
hourglass—and walk into an erg
                              (gravelled, no
grass: strange, someone whispers)
                    of silence
that spreads from the earth into my skin.

I see patches of memory, some tended
others bare; and a teaser drones
                    aimlessly
across

                    the horizon of my head
(while an Airbus 320 sprays graffiti
                    overhead):
          what tales does each one bear?

Then clouds of applause billow out
from a football match in Stade de France
and blow out all candles
          of thought for the night.

'Soundscapes' is a commissioned poem, part of a project spearheaded
by the city of Saint-Denis and Interstices, a local action group devoted
to renewing the image of this suburban city, once revered as the burial
ground for the kings of France and a primary centre of trade and
industry. So a set of writers and visual artists were asked to work in
pairs on predetermined themes: ours was architectural contrasts, and I
chose to work with the aural landscape.

    There was a strict brief on this piece: no formal verse, no rhyme, no
haiku, because it had to be translated into French and in a very short
span of time…

Snapshot on the Parisian Métro or Landscape on Line 3

Hinged between symmetric hips
(mom and maybe young aunt, arms
caressing packages from Printemps), the little boy
gapes at a soft navel studded
with curved barbells, 4 mm balls.
Its owner pores over Bourdieu's *L'amour de l'art*;
by her side, a grizzled guitarist
thrums a familiar tune or two while a strapholder
swings wildly to the metro's heavier drums,
a Nokia 256 and the London
Stock Exchange welded to one ear.
And the woman in white silk
nuzzling a mottled bouquet
closes her eyes, and smiles
from République to Parmentier.

Prelude

Day awakens, with parted lips,
stretches: lean limbs tracing
every curve on the skyline;
shrugs off the ragged quilt of dawn,
stands, poised—arms raised, feet flexed—
on the back of a passing moment;
then dives headlong into my loft
to scoop up lingering dreams.

But the shoals are no easy haul.
If I am up already—making
toast and tea or sipping history
straight from the spout
of a red-hot radio—and spot
the angler alight, we will tussle
over these trinkets left by Sleep,
shards sheltered among my lashes.

Then Day will murmur magic
morphemes, reveal the reason
for an early incursion.
And I, hearing the spell—or
was it a plea?—shall relent,
remove the treasure from its vault,
and watch as he flies
to a sleet-covered heap, sprinkling
the splinters on white wastes.
Out of the sudden thaw will flow
—red-skinned, reticent—another Spring.

Curriculum Vitae

Round them up, the ragtag team of movers
of time: loud-mouthed, burly moments stilling
breaths in swift embrace; weeks and months that stir,
rise—like faith in god, or a good maid—, last
or fade without trumpets; decades that spell
a new country, with lochs, crests and dales shaped

for all-terrain bikes or pilgrims. The shape
of the Nineties had seeped from r.e.m.
at daybreak after never-ending spells
of cramming; its myriad brash hues stilled
on VDUs that swiped sunsets those last
school years—high then graduate—when the stir

of the future drowned out countless unstirred
sermons by experts, survived the shapeless
omelettes and aged dal, then swore lasting
fealty in a rash of synchronized moves
across Mumbai, Chennai, their ilk, and, still
further, towns bodyshoppers couldn't spell

or map. Anti-gravity cast its spell:
we shot through the stratosphere, freshly stirred
petrichor lining pockets, and some stills
stowed-away in memory of odd shapes
and sounds from home: morning mantras moving
through rooms on wet feet; pageants by the last

monsoon clouds; ghazals whose echoes outlast
heartbreak... Early foes (eyeless crowds, spelling
bees with Immigration) stung as most moved
base (from simple present to the stirring
tales of future imperfect) to strobe shape-
shifting demons called y2k, or still

and stoke markets, even to coax stillness
to earth's ragged breath. We deejayed the last
beats of one millennium but shapely,
swaying lives somehow stepped into the spell
of quondam geekdom in the next, stirred
to *viable, dieable* age, a move

spelling limits, rebirth, changes, ends—shapes
that stir in the mind at night, like the last
movement of petrels over unstill seas.

Catalysts

It takes little to change
a life.
In the whisper of a breath,
in the echo of a smile;
tectonic plates, ocean currents,
cosmic forces that could
drive our destinies,
swing, bow and let through,
newness, transformation.
A spring of fresh clear water,
or a lee of verdant growth.
Maybe even a landmass, a continent.
Or disappearance: of arid wastelands,
swamps of dismay, even overrun
thickets of uncertainty?

They call it a catalyst.
A nimble spirit they seek everywhere,
in alchemy not the least.

And how would you greet that unsettling
tremor, the slight trigger etching out
glistening—unknown, unknowable, scary
but so desired—fresh lines on the palms
of fate's domineering hand?

Would it vanish in fear
if I turned around, and hailed
it with two puny words;
tried to convey all the beauty,
the glory, the pain of new-
found quests, of goals
emboldened, paths chosen
(not sprung, nor borne) with just
thank you?

Should I watch it cross these
thresholds with muted tread
from the curves of eyes,
and assume sightlessness
so it continues the spell?
Or polish the floor with rose-petals,
leave bowls of silent,
fragrant saffron—reward
and tempt at once in the hope
of regular returns?

Often though, I only learn
of a visit from damp footprints
outside my door, and a stir
in the air, spring unplanned
and unplugged.

The Revenant

It crosses uneven stretches
of oceans, mountains,
hemispheres. Time zones too.
Carpet-bombing quiet nights,
with raucous, ragged calls.
The music in your blood
flooding into tissues, neurons, bones;
a hum of familiar notes
threatening fealty beyond
memory, mortality.

The ache recedes.
You believe the self free.
A fistful of moments
when silence serenades
huddled spirits, tripping them
into a burst of flight.
Heady, spiralling
towards lost galaxies.
Stars playing catch
graze those cheeks.

Then collision.
Spin, out of orbit.
Rapid, heedless, the fall.
Hard earth opens its arms.
Home is thus.

Shards of you
scatter here, there, all about,
irretrievable, insignificant.
From the spine of the soil
and the dance of tired leaves
the melody resurges:
your lament once,
now the earth song.

The Invaders

Feasts and hallowed days spin on orbits
seldom grazing mine, till your voice swings
past meridians and meteorites
(Insat 2-B and Mobistar abetting)
this Saturday noon to hum *Happy Holi*
into the unwary whorls of a left eardrum.

I could weigh the vernal sunbeams
in those notes, bronzed on a bonfire
where good blooms in twice-born glee;
count the koel warming up behind—
the first chamber music concert this year
on a fourth-floor South Delhi balcony;
nearly touch flecks of gulaal tinting you
into a metonym for tropical spring.

The call ends, like other things.
But echoes of a koelled clarinet,
of your voice and its joyful salute,
snag on the woven blue rose stems
shading my kitchen window, perch on high
pelmets, recoil, reproduce and let
loose dissident whims:

To sift ochre, emerald, indigo
from the festive phonemes and smear
an ashen, unshaven sky above;

find water-balloons to hurl at chimney-potted
rooftops, a mass christening in cerise;

teach thumri to ungainly pigeons lumbering
on the girders outside—for a mehfil in mid-air....

I switch off the cell, and reheat tagliatelle
instead, adding paprika, pesto,
carrots and capsicum for a whisper
of insane flavour—it's Holi, after all.

Visitations: *Skype Warp*

A slice—uneven
—of chin, wild vermilion tracks
on a widow's peak,
two-dimensional manga
heads, voices in vibgyor

shimmy in and out
of place on a MacBook screen;
pixellate into parents,
a sporadic aunt,
peering gods and panting dog

blink-blinking aloud
in the sudden midnight sun
until eyes and emotions
find their feet, and tongues
rewire synapses, renew

the quest to connect;
mothers swift to slit
static, space and sentiment:
Your hair looks awful today,
do you go out looking this way?

Meridians

I

Half-past three in Vellayani: they are waking
the gods, one by one, with conch shells that blow off warm
quilts of hush, rose-water baths and sandalwood scrubs
for sludge from the hesternal pleas of devotees
and a half-open lotus for each pair of feet
while day awaits in damp muslin by the temple
doorway, dripping light—and early, unformed blessings
that cupped paternal hands collect with the same hope
you must have held the parchment etching my future
thirty-five harvests back; then carry down a mile
of winding belief (morning rustling underfoot),
tiptoeing home to lay them along a headboard
whence they trickle on the snowdrift of a pillow,
and seep through folds of igneous, agnostic dreams.

II

              Vieux Lyon, midnight overhead.
This is where I leave
(a mere vowel away from two coveted words):
a drunken, callow moon close at heel,
clattering
      down
           the humped
              cobblestones of Croix-Rousse;
I slip out through

                            an unseen traboule,
though the fragrance from your dreams
must linger in my breath
for he reappears (more surefooted),
catching up with me
      by the Saône.

RaceacrossPlaceBellecour –

s ^{t} e $_{e}$ p l e ^{c} ^{h} a $_{s}$ $_{i}$ n ^{g}
slogans stoned lovers
                installations
                    a few SDF
—to board the last noctambus,
but trip
on Louis XIV's elongated shade,

s
  c a   t   t
              e   r
    i
      n   g

a fistful of memories
over wet, red earth.
The moon, sober
from a dunk in the clouds,
steadies my thoughts and guides
feet up the hill that prays,
       his hand in mine all along
the ox-bow paths from Saints Jean to Just,

stopping

for a first kiss near the funiculaire,
one more
       for the road,
and another on the threshold: I let him be
(pretend it's you)
until he revs from gallant to persistent,
then slam
the door on long liquid fingers,
and pull down grey flannel blinds of sleep
on every window in my head.

III

In Wollongong, where land and sea rise in unbroken
swirls of colour and curve, you would stir early to catch
the blush from a kingfisher's breast, skim the horizon

for tender white clouds, line your bag with a cherished
    batch
of sour mango pickles, spray the rumour of spring tide
and the strum of unruly wheels (once—surprise!—a
    snatch

of a J.L. Seagull read by Richard Bach). Then ride
out fifty-one miles of rolling tarmac to Randwick
and that sterile square room in limp blue with a glad-eyed,

polka-dotted hippo on the floor to cheer homesick
teens from Trivandrum and their kin in crumpled cotton
and mien. Stride in like second life: with one hand, unpick

silence from tight chests; with the right, lob a ripened sun
for a plosion of tints, scents and words near-forgotten.

IV

I had never been to the Argentine
till last year: the evening your voice—soft pine
mostly, now and then a curtain of slate—
hurled a blizzard from that land. Then agate,
doubt, granite, frozen swells of mist and brine,

flakes of molten fear—all borne on the spine
of brittle words—crashed in ragged design
on my sphere, wrecking the early template
I have never been

able to sketch of our kinship since, fine
as cursives on a moth's wing, the outline
of dreams over sleeping seas. I'll conflate,
when old or mad, the word hell with this state:
swarthy earth and sulphur skies that opined
I had never been.

V

Moscow was different.
You went mute in Moscow: the city
spewed silence, a colourless
cavalry marching through
the air, invading throat and lung,
blitzing words before
they could flee past frontiers.

Later I learnt how General No—both
arm and anthem—had waterboarded every plea,
proof and argument you placed; would
transmute from verb to noun to idiom;
and materialize at airports, hotels,
banks and breakfast.

Two meridians away, I waited:
would have faced four days of pitch
quiet, utter disquiet rising
with Pethedine in frayed veins
somewhere in Le Chesnay—if
your fingers hadn't defected, sipped
syllables from a GSM, thrilled
to the taste of this draught, broken
bounds and tapped in turn.

Thence thought shuffled through,
numb at first, then in an outbreak
of soundless words. Tossed
via satellite, garbled by stray
bolts, retrieved—with arrogant ease—
through a mobile network, they sailed
into my head without knocking.

Half-dressed, dishevelled,
eager to dialogue and duel,
they filed onto shelves, counterpanes, brackets,
poised on pelmets, and danced:
dervished in fire and grace through dawn,
noon and dusk till we all heard
you had boarded hope
further east, then they floated
down like spent petals.

I picked them up and wrapped them
in pages of Plath, Eliot, Alvi
(left two within a Murakami),
packed my bags and caught
the next flight to Beijing.

VI

Then a caravan of cities, some swathed in night,
in monsoon's ashcloth, or blinds of celluloid light.
Hasty capitals, soft-footed towns like Roubaix:
their outlines beckon, elliptical, just in sight.

Some meet as would stars across galaxies—essay
distant courtesy; others, familiar-strange way-
farers at roadside inns, share a tale, a table;
some glare, with fears no papers nor prayers allay.

These polaroid impressions—single, unstable—
do we montage onto a family fable;
else catch their straying shadows and cast them in clay,
glass—or bronze, to make memories less friable.

So, Beijing, last spring, flew by in regal array—
Li Xinggang's bird's nest its crown of crimson and grey,
while we looped the endless realm of Terminal III
seeking ten mountain-born bamboo staves gone astray:

zigzagged a million square metres of duty free,
washrooms, walkways and sceptical security
(with two dancers and no Mandarin) to retrieve
peace, props and the future of choreography.

Berlin at summer's peak stood in standardized weave:
entre le chien et le loup all through, to grieve,
perhaps, its colours fled southwards for the solstice.
Obsidian night, tasselled with streets, could not reprieve

the uncut basalt of day, the relentless hiss
as rain exodussed from every interstice
in the sky—invading earth, skin, eyes, hair and thought.
That, with chocolate fountains and the midnight fizz

of critics champagning success on your myths, wrought
surreal shots—Burton-meets-Bushnell: you stood, taut,
Edward without scissorhands to slash through the frame
till Guy wielding humour, reduced the reels to nought.

Calais—or Douai? They both tend to smell the same
on wintry nights—of asphalt and mist, and the flame
(blue-eyed, bitter) from squat streetlamps that lie in wait
by doorways swollen with damp longing for a name

on their breastplates. No, it *was* Douai and a date
at its Hippodrome, where an End would generate
a crystal—hard-edged, painful—just below the heart.
One more ballet, unannounced, was to coruscate:

a few thousand red-tipped maple leaves, with upstart
ease, took centre-stage—Place du Barlet—to impart
fouettés, jetés, random entrechats … thus enthral
the roving streets, the stars above, an orphaned mart.

In November, Cannes secedes from the rest of Gaul.
With celestial skill, it churns a migrant Mistral:
pitchers of melted sunshine, pure, pounced cobalt
for sea and sky, garlands of palm trees (curtain-called

from summer) appear. Or so they say. With work's Alt
key activated, we must have missed heaven's vault:
a chauffeur awol with the sets, the untuned lyre,
no vegan meals in sight … there's little to exalt.

I find strands caught in a jacket, though, from sapphire
bights, the crew's laughter at 2 a.m., awestruck tiers
and ovation. *Au 'voir*, then, not *adieu,* despite
this awkward tryst: next time, I'll leave behind the ire.

VII

The very first day I learnt
I could unleash my eyes in Dengfeng.
Remove the hood of French Reserve and soar in glee.
Unchain my gaze from the pavement,
aim it straight at strangers.
Let both eyes free fly in a lobby.
Dive through private doorways, glide past curtains.
Linger on faces—fresh or familiar
(spent hours tracking the sun
scrawl and erase cursives
on your four sleeping profiles,
their cheeks, their ears, a chin).
Crash mid-air into other stares—unabashed,
unblinking—cartographing the eight
aimless freckles on my forehead,
a left hand and its absent gold band.
'Né-hao', we would smilingly say,
with none of the eyes shying away.

The second morning we went
by the town's cascades of sound
for a quick collective plunge.
A few scrambled back tout de suite,
spluttering, spitting—out fell pebbled
car-horns, gravel from karaoke clubbers,
sea-drifts of public loudspeakers.

A bit of blood was drawn: ears splintered
by slivers from giant cement mixers,
a couple of throats grazed as well
thanks to caterwauling wayside vendors.
Some stayed longer, swimming with the spring
tide of decibels, headed upstream
into the main street and returned,
dripping delight and reddish-brown furor
on the hotel's just-washed marble floor.

It took a little longer to uncover
each individual member
of the secret service of scents,
infiltrating all outsiders, spreading
battle-hardened tentacles from rain
to skin to memory, and breeding
double and triple agents of every strain.
Green, White, Wulong, Pu-erh,
Guanyin and crushed Sunflower,
the teas enrolled straight from the infantry
blew silently to foster habit.
The dancing girls—jasmine, lotus, wisteria,
sliced bamboo, the ghost of last year's magnolia—
tripped in and out, not seen but smelt,
and stayed, some curled between clavicles,
one beneath a left auricle.
The first directorate of odours,
with no time for suchlike subterfuge,
hammered streets, gardens and the marketplace,
with shredded betel, dried pee and turd,
waves of old sweat; worn earth, rice liquor, moist

concrete and menstrual blood
came in for the rearguard thrust.

It had all felt oddly tried and tasted, love-hated:
the sounds, the smells, my own reflexes.
Six weeks later, on a far hemisphere,
I woke up wearing your borrowed lenses,
the fading notion: had it been less monochrome,
I might have mistaken Dengfeng for home.

Homestay, Schaerbeek

I had forgotten that houses talk.

This one finds me amusing, I think. There is a regular, sleepy rumble of laughter—affectionate, not scornful—from floorboards and rafters that seem to rouse themselves from time to time by watching the gauche choreography of my hausfrauly activity on an unfamiliar stage: setting the dishwasher on, chewing over the identical knobs of a gas fire (my mind comes to a skittish halt in front of them just as my mother's body does before escalators), the tug of war with a recalcitrant house key that jams much as Bogdan predicted it would (despite our trial runs yesterday), and the irate rummage for a knife to slice meat.

I had not considered becoming entertainment for a gracious building but, well, we all have uses other than those we pride ourselves on.

A brassy grandfather clock chimes in contrapuntal regularity to my fingers on the keyboard, benign reminder of the day that's packing up its bag of tools, rubbing out the hopscotch game the six identical skylights overhead had sketched out for me on ecru floorboards.

An occasional whisper as a north-easterly breeze flirts with the lonesome sword lily standing by the terrace, chaperoned only by a lion cub marbled into immobility—and boredom.

A windowpane rattles, but discreetly.

All other sounds have been exiled. In some other time zone, there is the tuneless laughter of children and a siren wailing in desperation. Somewhere, too, a reggae beat is winding its way towards the heart of Brussels. About seventy feet below, there is an entire sonic galaxy thriving.

But Bogdan left strict orders to his loft, I think, just as he did to the day: provide the right settings for writing, no distractions, no disturbance. No rain to torpedo thought, no reverberating beats of *I AM* from the flat below. Everything— even the beam against which my head rests as I lean on the wall and type on my lap—is made to measure.

He didn't realize, I am sure, that the house would cast such a spell, decide to become actor instead of décor. Writing should be simple here. There is no ruthless struggle with the world at large fighting for attention. Yet, all I want to do is listen to it, ask it questions, hear the tales it hums by morning, learn why it has this air of omniscience, of poised good humour, and discover how it can transform me from impatient Parisian to a long-discarded teenage self. Fill me with the forgotten sense of diffidence at moving in new territory; the awareness of being assessed on yardsticks other than those that rule over my planet.

And—this is new, though—the total acceptance of these rules.

It feels subversive too: breaking deadlines, switching off

alarms, deactivating mobile phones (oh, unutterable horror!), eating at will...

Maybe I won't have written at all at the end of the day.

Maybe I won't care.

ACKNOWLEDGEMENTS

Acknowledgements are due to the editors of the following publications:

Indian Literature (May–June 2007), the journal of Sahitya Akademi, edited by A.J. Thomas, which first published 'Afterwards', 'Blueprint', 'Interregnum', 'Pillowtalk', and 'Visiting Hours I, II & III'

60 Indian Poets, edited by Jeet Thayil (Penguin Books India 2008), which published 'Interregnum', 'Snapshot on the Parisian Metro or Landscape on Line 3', 'Visiting Hours I, II & III', and 'Zero Degrees: Between Boundaries'

The Bloodaxe Book of Contemporary Indian Poets, edited by Jeet Thayil (Bloodaxe, 2008), which published 'Interregnum', 'Snapshot on the Parisian Metro or Landscape on Line 3', 'Visiting Hours I, II & III', and 'Zero Degrees: Between Boundaries'

Saint-Denis, portraits sensibles (éditions Magellan/Interstices, 2008), for 'Soundscapes in Saint-Denis'

The Literary Review (guest edited by Sudeep Sen, summer 2009) and *Atlas*

In 'Distant Music', the opening phrases of each movement are from poems of W.S. Graham: 'Gently disintegrate me' from

'Enter a Cloud' (1977); 'I leave this at your ear for when you wake' from 'I Leave This at Your Ear' (1970); and 'Imagine a forest' from 'Imagine a Forest' (1977).

In 'Curriculum Vitae', the phrase 'viable, dieable' is from Arundhati Roy's novel *The God of Small Things* (1997).

My thanks to

Paul Zacharia: the first catalyst, for guidance and belief.

V.K. Karthika: for this unimagined opportunity; for freedom, trust and quiet support.

Anita Roy: for sparking connections with people and words, for generosity of time and thought.

A.J. Thomas, Jeet Thayil, Mita Kapur, Grégory Lavacherie & Marie-Caroline de Baecque, Priya Sarukkai Chabria: for plinths and platforms.

Girija Kaimal, Sankar Mohan Radhakrishnan, Martine Depagniat, Philippe Bruguière, Jean-Philippe Echard, Bogdan Batic: comrades-in-arms, for honesty, cheer and acceptance, amused or resigned.

Arthur Nauzyciel, Mathew Kallumkal, Dominique Vitalyos, Jayshree Menon, Szymon Brzóska, Patrice Martinet, Sarada Muraleedharan, Antony Gormley, Sanjoy Roy: the truth-seekers, for their readings.

Dr Claudine Blanchet-Bardon, Anne-Christine Degut, Paulette Malaval: for knowledge, hope and care.

Shantanu Ray Chaudhuri and Shuka Jain of HarperCollins: for patience and attention.

Sidi Larbi Cherkaoui: prime meridian, for creating language with movement, and this time, with colours and cursives.

Caleb Custer: for his skill and generosity.

Achan-Amma and Renaud: for sustenance.